J   Gilleo, Alma
387
Gil   Water travel from
           the beginning

DATE DUE

Discard

WATER TRAVEL
from the Beginning

by Alma Gilleo
illustrated by John Nelson

THE CHILD'S WORLD

ELGIN, ILLINOIS 60120

Distributed by Childrens Press, 1224 West Van Buren Street, Chicago, Illinois 60607.

Library of Congress Cataloging in Publication Data
Gilleo, Alma, 1920-
  Water travel from the beginning.
  SUMMARY: A history of water travel discussing the first log boats, early ships, and present-day vessels.
  1. Navigation—History—Juvenile literature. 2. Ships—History—Juvenile literature. [1. Navigation—History. 2. Ships—History]
I. Nelson, John, 1928- II. Title.
VK15.G54   387   77-22822
ISBN 0-89565-001-0

In the early days, the only way to travel was by foot. But how could people cross water? There were no boats or bridges. Probably people waded or swam across small streams. But how could they cross wide rivers? Or lakes?

The first thing man used for water travel was probably a log. Perhaps someone used the log to help him as he swam. He could tie his things to the log. Then he learned that he could sit on the log. He could paddle with his hands.

Later, a pole was used to push the log across the water. Logs made it easier to cross rivers.

Soon, though, people wanted a better way to cross rivers. Someone learned how to make a raft by tying several logs together with strong vines. He used a pole to push the raft across small streams. Later, someone made paddles to use in deep water.

Some people thought of a way to make a raft float better. They filled sheep or goat skins with air. They tied them under their raft. These rafts didn't tip over so easily. But they were harder to steer.

Rafts are still used today in some parts of the world. Would you like to ride on a raft?

Raft with skins
tied under it

After rafts, came boats. What did the first boat look like? No one knows. Probably someone cut or dug or burned wood out of a log. He made a dugout. A person could sit in his dugout and paddle across the water.

People learned to make other kinds of small boats too. The outrigger was a smart idea. It was a small boat with long poles sticking out from one side. A log was fastened to the poles. The log kept the boat from tipping over.

Eskimos made a boat called a kayak. It was made of bone instead of wood. It had a skin covering over the top. The covering had a hole in it. The Eskimo sat in this hole.

American Indians had still another small boat, the birchbark canoe. It was made of wood and covered with bark.

A kayak

An outrigger

A birchbark canoe

The first boats larger than canoes may have been made in Egypt. The Egyptians cut planks or boards from trees to make boats. The trees were small, so the planks were short. They were fastened together with wood pegs.

By this time, people had learned that the wind could help push boats along. So the Egyptians made sails that the wind could easily blow. They put them on their ships. A tall pole in the center of a ship held the sail. When there was no wind, men used paddles to move the boat.

Some rich people in Egypt had their own small boats. They were like the boat in the top picture. See the big paddles. The bottom picture shows a bigger boat with a large sail. It took many men to paddle this boat.

8

Soon other people were building large boats too. Some of the best builders were the Phoenicians.

The Phoenicians were traders and very good sailors. They sailed to many countries. They went to places where no other strangers had ever gone. Some people think they sailed all the way around Africa.

These people also built warships called galleys. The picture shows how one galley may have looked. The oars were very long—probably more than 40 feet. Six strong men worked each one.

The Greeks and Romans also had many merchant ships and war galleys.

A Phoenician galley

The Phoenicians, the Greeks, and the Romans built good ships. But then the Vikings started building ships. And their ships were better. For the Vikings had to sail on the stormy North Atlantic Sea.

A Viking longship was strong but light, and very fast. Vikings learned how to sail against the wind. No one else had learned that yet.

A Viking longship was made of large planks, or boards. It had a large square sail. Oars were placed in holes along the ship's side.

The Viking ships were sometimes called Dragon ships. Can you guess why? What would you think if you saw a Dragon ship headed for your town? If you knew it was filled with strong, fierce warriors? People everywhere were afraid when they saw the Viking longships.

Viking longships

Even the Viking ships traveled close to land or from island to island. But soon, men wanted to know what was beyond the oceans. To cross rough seas, they needed better ships.

So people made new kinds of sails. One was a triangle-shaped sail. People put it on a mast that leaned forward. It was called a lateen sail. This sail is still used on some ships today.

But one sail was not enough. Soon ships had more sails. The ship in the picture is called a square-rigger. It has three masts and many sails. This ship could cross the rough ocean. Columbus sailed to the new world in a ship like this one.

A square-rigger

By this time, countries were sending ships to cities far away. They sent them to buy tin, food, and other things. They sent goods to sell to other countries also. Some ships carried people to other cities and countries.

But travel by boat was not easy in the early days. There were no modern kitchens on the ships. Bread was dry. Other food often spoiled. A hundred people might be crowded together. If one got sick, others usually got sick, too. There was no comfortable place to sleep, no place to run or play.

Travel was slow, even on the best ships. The *Mayflower* sailed from England to America in 1620. The trip took 66 days. Today ships can make the trip in just five days.

The *Mayflower* reaches America.

Many different kinds of ships were made in the next 200 years. All of them needed the wind to push them across the water.

By this time, steam engines were being used to move trains. Why couldn't they move boats? Some men thought they could.

A steamboat began to run on the Hudson River in 1807. Robert Fulton planned it. The steam engine turned a paddle wheel on the side of the boat. The paddles pushed the boat through the water. People liked to ride on Mr. Fulton's steamboat.

Soon there were many steamboats in America.

About 30 years later, a steamship from England crossed the ocean. Now men did not have to worry about wind power. They could use steam power to cross the oceans.

Robert Fulton and his steamboat *Clermont*

People kept making better and better ships. The early steamships were made of wood. Soon England began making ships of iron. A little later, people made ships of steel.

Someone invented a propeller for ships. It pushed a ship faster than the paddle wheel could.

People made better engines too. One was the Diesel engine. Even today, many ships use the Diesel engine, which burns oil.

With better engines, people could build bigger ships. Today, large ships carry oil and other goods.

Large ships, like the one in the picture, carry people. These ships are like giant hotels. They have many bedrooms, dining rooms, and shops. They even have swimming pools.

An ocean liner

As men learned to travel on top of the water, they wanted to go under the sea too. About 350 years ago, a man built an underwater boat. It was a wood boat covered with skins. Oars were pushed into tight holes in the skins. Twelve men rowed this boat under water.

The boat did not go very deep. It couldn't. But it was the first submarine that worked. Later, better submarines were made, submarines that would go deep under water.

Still, people wanted to go much deeper. They wanted to go to the bottom of the ocean. Nearly 50 years ago, the bathysphere was invented. People on board a ship let the bathysphere down into the ocean. Finally, men could see what was on the ocean floor.

Submarines are very useful for finding enemy ships during a war. They are also used in exploring. In 1958, the United States used a new kind of power in a submarine. It was nuclear power. The name of the submarine is *Nautilus*. Its picture is on the next page.

This new submarine could stay under water for a long time. It did not have to come up for air as others did.

Two years later, the *Triton*, another nuclear submarine, went around the world under water. It took 84 days.

Nuclear power can be used on other kinds of ships too. Nuclear ships are the fastest ships in the world. But they cost so much money, even large companies do not buy them. And it takes a long time to train men to run one.

The *Nautilus*

About the time the nuclear submarine was made, a man in England was working on a new kind of boat. His boat was a kind of flying boat. It traveled on air above the water. It is called a Hovercraft.

The boat you see in the picture is a Hovercraft. Fans suck in air at the top of the boat. Other fans force the air out at the bottom. That force of air lifts the boat off the water. Propellers move the boat.

Today, Hovercrafts carry people across the channel between England and France. Maybe someday Hovercrafts will be used in many other countries. Wouldn't you like to ride on a flying boat?

Today there are all kinds of boats and ships on rivers and oceans all around the world.

There are fast motor boats and slow sailboats, large ocean liners and small canoes. There are fireboats and tugboats. There are even some boats used for homes. These are called house-boats.

Have you ever been in a boat? What kind? Have you taken a ride in a speedboat like the one in the picture? Maybe your family has taken the car on a ferry boat across a river.

Today there is a boat or ship for every need. Some travel to far away countries. Some are just for fun, near home.

People are still working on new ways to travel on or under water. Others want to find new ways to study the sea.

One of these people is Jacques Cousteau. He built a station for sea divers. He called it *Conshelf*. *Conshelf* II rested under 36 feet of water. Five divers lived in it for a month. They could swim out of the station to explore the sea.

Others built stations too. The U.S. Navy built *Sealab* I in 1964. Astronaut M. Scott Carpenter helped to test it. *Sealab* II rested 205 feet deep in the Pacific Ocean.

The picture, though, is not of *Conshelf* or *Sea-lab*. It is simply a picture of what one artist thinks might happen under water in the future.

30

Would you want to live in an underwater colony like this one?

What do you think will happen? Do you think people will live on the ocean floor? Will they have farms in the ocean? What do you think would grow there?

What do you think will happen in water travel? Maybe someone will find a way to make nuclear power ·that does not cost so much money. Or perhaps someone will make a new kind of ship.

No one knows what will happen in the future. But people like to think about it and dream about it. They dream just as people once dreamed of crossing oceans and of traveling under the sea.